REPOSE IN THE METROPOLIS

The Private Gardens of New York City

REPOSE IN THE METROPOLIS

The Private Gardens of New York City

BY LISA ZEIGER
FOREWORD BY MITCHELL OWENS

SCHIFFER
PUBLISHING

4880 Lower Valley Road • Atglen, PA 19310

Designed by Molly Shields

Covers, Title Page, and Contents: Kim Hoyt, photos by Dan Wonderly
This page: Brook Klausing, photo by Brook Klausing
Epigraph (p. 6) and Foreword (p. 11): Stephen Eich, photos by Hollander Design Landscape Architects
Introduction (p. 12): Thomas Woltz, photo by Eric Piasecki

Type set in Effra/Miller Text

ISBN: 978-0-7643-6602-4

Printed in China

Published by Schiffer Publishing, Ltd.
4880 Lower Valley Road
Atglen, PA 19310
Phone: (610) 593-1777; Fax: (610) 593-2002
Email: Info@schifferbooks.com
Web: www.schifferbooks.com

For our complete selection of fine books on this and related subjects, please visit our website at www.schifferbooks.com. You may also write for a free catalog.

Schiffer Publishing's titles are available at special discounts for bulk purchases for sales promotions or premiums. Special editions, including personalized covers, corporate imprints, and excerpts, can be created in large quantities for special needs. For more information, contact the publisher.

We are always looking for people to write books on new and related subjects. If you have an idea for a book, please contact us at proposals@schifferbooks.com.

For Petra Grunert Singh,
flower child in Harlem

Here, at last, I should find that low door in the wall which others, I knew, had found before me, which opened on an enclosed and enchanted garden, which was somewhere, not overlooked by any window in the heart of that gray city.

—Evelyn Waugh, *Brideshead Revisited*

CONTENTS

FOREWORD BY MITCHELL OWENS 10

INTRODUCTION: STRANGER IN PARADISE 12

WALKS OF LIFE Michael Van Valkenburgh 14

BRONZE REPOSE Billie Cohen 20

ONE WAY OR ANOTHER Kim Hoyt 28

DIPTYCH David Kelly
Rees Roberts + Partners 44

LANDED Stephen Eich
Hollander Design Landscape Architects 56

GREEN MANSIONS Michael Trapp 70

ABOVE ALL Julie Farris
XS Space 76

ON THIS ROCK Steven Tupu,
terrain-nyc 92

THE SEEDS OF STYLE Brook Klausing 102

FOR THE BIRDS Thomas Woltz,
Nelson Byrd Woltz Landscape Architects 114

FOREWORD

BY MITCHELL OWENS

Lisa Zeiger is a formidable scholar of the decorative arts, and her intellectual world has long been an interior one, taking the measure of the vessel-like sculptures of Andrew Lord, the paintings of Edward Burne-Jones, even the mesmerizing rooms in which she has lived here, there, and everywhere. Most notable among them was an apartment in Glasgow that appeared in *The World of Interiors* in 1993, which is likely the first time I came across her name and was introduced to her romantic aesthetic.

Several years later, Lisa and I crossed paths in Manhattan. We had both become contributors to *Nest*, the spiritually psychedelic cult shelter magazine founded in 1997 by Joseph Holtzman. It startled the cognoscenti, illuminated the bizarrely beautiful, upended conventional notions of art direction, and confounded its newsstand competitors before ending its brilliant, blasphemous, bobsled run after six years. In an early editorial meeting, or perhaps it was a cocktail party—at *Nest* they often seemed to be one and the same—Lisa turned my head. Her off-kilter Pre-Raphaelite beauty, all-tumbling locks, proud profile, enormous eyes, drawling voice, and fierce intelligence reminded me of Lady Ottoline Morrell, the bohemian hostess of the Bloomsbury years. She was also kind, funny, a trifle chaotic, bracingly candid, and an unsettlingly skilled writer. Whether it was an examination of the sexually charged hobbies of Italian architect Carlo Mollino or the shopaholic pathology of First Lady Mary Todd Lincoln, Lisa's articles stunned us all with their depth of knowledge, their easy eloquence, the ability to dig deep beneath surface prettiness and aesthetic novelty to find another story, the real story, one that fascinated as often as it discomfited. Her articles for *Nest* and other publications—among them *Apollo* and the *Art Newspaper*—filled me with envy as well as a determination to write better and deeper rather than merely skating lyrically over a subject in order to meet the next deadline.

Small wonder that Lisa was one of the magazine's most resonant voices, as important to the *Nest* DNA as Joe or his husband, Carl Skoggard, himself a writer of great power and memorable charm. Now, I am pleased to report, her friends and fans come face to face with her latest work—*Repose in the Metropolis: The Private Gardens of New York City*. My former colleague and dear friend has left the nest, as it were, and strolled into the sunlight, bringing her observational talents and intrepid musings to bear on the wondrous vagaries of Mother Nature and a number of landscape architects and designers, maestros of the vegetal world. From an Upper East Side townhouse plot devised by Stephen Eich, to a Chelsea penthouse terrace by Michael Trapp, to a Japan-themed Brooklyn garden by Kim Hoyt, to many more, the landscapes herein reveal the softer side of an overpopulated, overbuilt, haphazardly worked archipelago that can seem adamantine, unyielding, even heartless.

Urban gardens are challenged landscapes, to say the least, no matter how beautiful they are to the naked eye. Especially in Manhattan and the boroughs that surround that legendary isle like a batch of pups, a realm that has been in flux since its founding and whose institutional attempts to green the grid have been arguably undernourished. Even exceptional gardens are periodically threatened, such as British genius Russell Page's mignon 1970s masterpiece at the Frick Collection. Like that space, now blessedly preserved after public outrage, the intimate landscapes that Lisa wanders through in *Repose in the Metropolis*, whether intended for one person's private delectation or for a community of neighbors in need of relief from the hubbub of the streets, are relatively small, at least in comparison with Central Park and Prospect Park, those magnificent swards that belong to all New Yorkers and that, in their way, serve as spiritual guides to every local householder with a bit of earth to turn and to tend.

That being said, as Lisa observes and every landscape designer understands, even the most bucolic city garden is forced to defend itself. Bedeviled by the heat radiating from sun-baked masonry. Chilled by the dense shadows cast by buildings that tower above and around. Coaxed out of concrete-hard soil that must be broken up and be made fertile through many an efficacious application. But survive they do, and, as *Repose in the Metropolis* proves, thrive they have. Some of the gardens that Lisa surveys are perched atop high buildings, where they are raked by winds and seared by the sun, yet they remain lush and heart-catching, places of refuge and rejuvenation. Others hug the earth, tucked into damp recesses wherein few things would seem able to thrive, but somehow they do just that, with fern fronds uncoiling in the manner of verdant lace, and ivy leaves glistening like tridents of polished jadeite, relieved by high-borne blossoms of blue and white and lilac.

Contemporary evocations of our ancestral Eden, usually humble; sometimes grand, speckle the boroughs, diverting eyes and feeding souls. One hopes that this book will lead readers to cultivate their own *hortus conclusus*, a private spot where one can turn inward and find calm, contemplation, and contentment and return to the workaday world refreshed. Andrew Marvell perhaps described it best in his elegiac poem "The Garden" (1681), in which he described his yearning for a place where "My soul into the boughs does glide; / There like a bird it sits and sings, / Then whets, and combs its silver wings; / And till prepar'd for longer flight / Waves in its plumes the various light." With Lisa Zeiger as your guide, *Repose in the Metropolis* takes you there.

Mitchell Owens is the American editor of
The World of Interiors

INTRODUCTION

Stranger in Paradise

A garden is the most complex art form on earth, and beauty is the least of it.

I began this book in December 2020, the end of one plague year and the eve of another. COVID-19 had made New York City into a shock corridor of empty streets, masked breath, and frantic handwashing. Avoidance replaced connection; eyes took on a new allure. So did gardens and, if you didn't have one, houseplants.

My own life barely changed; now everyone lived it! I was happy as always to sit at home writing about images of rooms, artworks, and now gardens. After decades fixated on the decoration of houses, I went outdoors at last, pried from my pillows by a disease.

From monographs, anthologies, treatises, coffee-table books, and first-person accounts of how a particular garden came to be, I found that almost any book by a garden designer is, in some sense, a memoir. At Christmas a friend gave me Russell Page's 1962 classic *The Education of a Gardener*, a book that brought the legendary English designer fame that has outlasted his gardens, though each was a new triumph of invention and nuance. Next I read *Home Ground: Sanctuary in the City*, by Dan Pearson, England's most influential garden designer from the 1990s onward. Published in 2011, Pearson's essays form a seasonal diary of how he patiently brought to full bloom a bleak, neglected plot in South London. I still leaf through *The Writer in the Garden*, Jane Garmey's treasury of sixty-three essays and poems by famous writer-gardeners, from Alexander Pope to Vita Sackville-West; Gertrude Jekyll to M. F. K. Fisher. (Historically, women who wrote about gardens have been published more steadily than those who wrote novels.)

On the magic lantern of Instagram, gardens filed past me for ten hours a day, as reported by a graph on my iPhone. I saw America's first designs, her wild places; the ceremonious paths and outdoor salons that emanate from European chateaux; and England's charming vernacular gardens fraught with follies or ramshackle sheds. On Instagram, all the images had informative captions written with wit by scholars who wore their learning lightly. Trails of handles and hashtags led from one gifted designer to the next; I stalked four of them right into this book.

First responders to our overbuilt times, garden designers toil to replenish the indigenous plants, trees, birds, and pollinators of New York's prehistory. They find in native plants an ecologically sound path of least resistance toward sustainability that fits. Their unforced aesthetic brings to mind four words: *Beauty Looks After Herself*, title of a 1933 book by the English artist-typographer Eric Gill.

Every garden is the biography of a small piece of the earth, its prehistoric bedrock encrusted with centuries of discarded styles and technologies. The existing trees, plants, and architectural elements of a plot may obstruct a designer's ideal, but it is just such inconveniences that give a site its roots. A designer's most difficult site is a bulldozed lot, a ghost that lingers amid luxuriant new trees, shrubs, grasses, and flowers.

The indoor spaces I've loved for so long are set in their ways, whereas gardens and landscapes, growing or dying, catch beauty on the hoof. A garden is not a throne room. It's a road trip.

In renewing a garden, as in changing our lives, we can never start over. But, in the nick of time, we can begin.

WALKS OF LIFE
MICHAEL VAN VALKENBURGH

"Nature doesn't care what we do," observes landscape architect Michael Van Valkenburgh.

The love we lavish on gardens is unrequited; a one-sided passion for an unpredictable beauty who, like Greta Garbo, just wants to be alone.

Michael is the founder of a large practice with offices in New York City and Boston. Among his team are his former students from the Graduate School of Design at Harvard University, where he has taught since 1982 and is now the Charles Eliot professor emeritus of practice.

On the West and East Coasts, and across America's untold striations between them, Michael invents new urban parks, loosens up old formal grounds at historic universities, and humbly contributes to the protection and vitality of forests, marshlands, and wildlife preserves. He is especially famous for landscapes surrounding America's most important museums. They contrast dramatically in era and architecture, from the 1903 Isabella Stewart Gardner Museum in Boston, to Renzo Piano's brilliant building for the highly idiosyncratic Menil Collection in Houston, which opened in 1987.

Photography: Michael Van Valkenburgh Associates

Willow Street Garden

Eclipsed by Michael's sweeping public commissions is another repertoire: nearly secret gardens he designs for private houses, many on the East Coast, such as Willow Street Garden. Behind a five-story brownstone in Brooklyn Heights, a long flight of stairs connects the backyard to a small upper terrace no deeper than a balcony. Michael describes the whole site as "a curiosity shaped by the dramatic grades of Brooklyn Heights." Michael implanted another green world into his invented microclimate, cooler than the outside world in summer, warmer in winter.

From the terrace, the steep black metal stairs descend to the irregular backyard. Darkened by other houses, it was enclosed on two sides by a 12-foot-tall red-brick wall of great age and character, but unstable, as such things always are. Michael's team stabilized the nineteenth-century enclosure with engineered columns.

Another nineteenth-century relic was an abandoned rain cistern covered with ramshackle plywood planks. Michael's team repurposed the cistern as a vessel for stormwater runoff from the brownstone's roof and garden. Excess water now flows into the cistern, seeping gradually into the water table.

To the left of the stairs is a narrow space perpendicular to the main garden. Michael unified the two areas by paving them in silvery mica schist, which traces a contiguous path through the L-shaped ground. In doing so, he reshaped the rectangular lower garden into a partially open-sided hexagon with contours loosely demarcated by the oblong pavers. Like the "crazy paving" first used in ancient Rome, the stepping-stones vary in length and width, slant in all directions, and do not touch. Separated by wide seams of earth, the scattershot paving is "floating,

animated, and unresolved," he says. He arranged crape myrtle trees at spacious, irregular intervals, with smaller plantings such as camellias and vines emerging in unexpected places.

Michael's paths are his signature. He describes Willow Street as "a journey, a descent," a garden whose meaning is movement: "Going down the stairs is a delight."

In the winter of 1974 the German film director Wim Wenders walked from Munich to Paris to see a dying friend, each of his footsteps an incantation to save her life. She lived. Decades later, Wenders gave a lecture at Stanford about the experience, with the title "The World Reveals Itself to Those Who Walk."

Michael Van Valkenburgh lives and works and walks as if possessed by Wenders's declaration, designing gardens that incite in visitors an irresistible impulse to "get up and move." They do.

Within the closed, fragrant world of Willow Street, the owners and their guests walk through unstudied clusters of trees, grasses, and flowering plants. Michael Van Valkenburgh prefers gardens with unperfected views, cut through by a path; the slow road to pleasures without time.

Michael Van Valkenburgh, master of the quixotic, brought this fractured, rather dark multilevel backyard to an unexpected state of grace. At far left is the black metal staircase that descends the steep grade from a tiny upper terrace to the loosely hexagonal garden below. "Going down a flight of stairs into the garden is a journey, a descent—a delight!" Michael's irregularly scattered pavers of mica schist creates "a sense of floating and animation rather than resolute grounding. The larger lower garden centers on a large crape myrtle with arborvitae, an evergreen, scattered throughout.

The photo (*at left*) and the drawn plan (*above*) illustrate Michael's desire to lead us down the garden path—or in his case, paths—that in the proverb may lead to places one doesn't necessarily want to go. The schematic drawing at right is a rounded kaleidoscope housing hidden paths teased out among oblong pavers all aslant, with bare ground in between. Note at left the ancient retaining brick wall now fortified by engineered columns.

BRONZE REPOSE
BILLIE COHEN

Manhattan landscape designer Billie Cohen is a master at connecting plants and trees to rarefied architectural materials until they reach an ideal relationship she calls "the "angle of repose."

Billie began her life in garden design as a fine artist, learning from painting how to integrate the two-dimensional world. "Every time you put a stroke of color on the canvas, you create a new spatial, compositional problem to be resolved. There was a distinct moment, painting landscapes, when I realized, 'I want to do that'—to grapple with the three-dimensional." Billie went to horticultural school at the New York Botanical Gardens in the Bronx, an intense training in gardening, in the soil, and in the total habitat of plants, including the architecture of the site. Her eventual training in landscape architecture was the final step of her long education.

The title "Bronze Repose" is borrowed from a phrase in W. B. Yeats's 1928 poem "Among School Children."

Photography by David Sundberg

Upper West Side Hermitage

A recent project enacts Billie's angle of repose in the tiny backyard of a nine-teenth-century limestone townhouse on the Upper West Side. Its tall, solemn rooms have intricate wood moldings and stained-glass panels and transoms. Dark wood paneling in the original kitchen was brightened by old bronze hardware, including a burnished hood above the stove. The bronze stayed in Billie's mind as a material that could visually connect the interior to the outdoor space. The unpromising site originally "was never meant to be seen," used in the past by servants to wash laundry and hang it out to dry. Its walls of concrete blocks were covered in a broken wooden fence. Billie's first thought was "I don't want to replace a broken fence; I want to build walls for a room."

The owners desired a garden only to improve the forlorn view from the kitchen windows. As Billie sketched out various spatial arrangements, she suggested that it should be lived in as well as seen. When COVID arrived in 2020, indoor rooms were suddenly too close for company. Billie's proposal was now a necessity her clients took up with alacrity.

Interestingly, it was the once-grim view from this kitchen window that inspired Billie's clients to have it frame a verdant, flowery tableau. The existing backyard was not a garden at all, but a space, in earlier times, to hang laundry. It had become an insalubrious jumble of concrete slabs, derelict fencing, and unsightly buildings next door. Billie's original brief was to create a new view, but gradually the small yard cried out to be used as well as seen. The elegant bronze fence and sleek modern furniture now enclose family and friends in a quintessential "green room."

In collaboration with the contractor, Billie determined that the fence should be replaced with a bronze wall, transforming the space into a beautiful room. The clients plunged in. The transformation began by improving the humble back facade to be, in effect, the garden's fourth wall. Billie removed the metal security gates over windows and doors along with piping and cable boxes. The facade was detailed with new window frames and sills, pilasters that cover cables, and an overhead bay window clad in copper panels. Three stately 8-foot walls now block neighbors' backyards from sight.

The walls are majestic, rich, and very somber. Billie divided them horizontally into a 6-foot-high dado surmounted by a 2-foot frieze. She lightened the ponderous dado with panels that are slightly recessed and framed by classical molding. The 2-foot frieze is modern and light, pierced with rows of small ovals that stream narrow beams of sunlight into the yard. The north wall incorporates a dark mirror on one panel to extend the space. On the east wall, the panel is mounted with a bronze rod with a twist of rope, handmade by the contractor. Along the perimeter, an existing concrete floor was dug out to install evergreen hedges with a dogwood tree in one corner. The contractor laid a floor of gleaming white porcelain tiles.

Now handsomely fortified, the garden room called for ethereal plantings. Billie's palette used broadleaf evergreen as a dark background for the white-flowering cherry laurel and dogwood. She added white hellebore and white ranunculus, a delicate contrast to the clients' pots of pink azaleas, her favorite flower. Boston ivy was trained to climb the twisted ropes. The owner became a convert to the monochromatic white-blooming plants when she saw how the flowers glowed in the evening,

The owners have traditional tastes, so Billie was surprised when they chose a modernist-inspired collection of outdoor furniture from Minotti. The sofa and chairs, upholstered in taupe, are poised on slender bronze legs, with the arms and

Above left, the bronze wall serves as a canvas for a palette of dark broadleaf evergreen highlighted by white-flowering cherry laurel, white ranunculus, and white hellebore. *Above right*, the clients' favorite flower, pink azaleas.

back forming a single curving shell of skinny bronze spindles. The seats are large in proportion to the space, a reminder of legendary decorator Billy Baldwin's tip: to make a small room feel bigger, fill it with large pieces of furniture.

Billie's use of bronze brings to mind the buildings and interiors of the Italian architect Carlo Scarpa, perhaps her greatest influence. In the 1950s and '60s, Scarpa built massive iconoclast structures from rough or polished concrete, with elegant, expansive facings of marble, terrazzo, or cast bronze. Scarpa's final project, the Brion Cemetery, is sometimes described as his manifesto. "An architect friend took me to Venice to visit Scarpa's cemetery," Billie says. "Cornfields were all around it, and the corn went to the end of the sight line. Inside the mausoleum there was a trench along its perimeter, and a tilted wall. The lawn was floating. You knew you were supposed to see it at that moment."

Like Scarpa, Billie ennobles her gardens with materials mined from the depths and excrescences of the earth. The protective artifice of this garden room serves the many lives inside. Its exuberant plants and flowers, stalked by birds and insects, are the wild cards of human dominion.

Opposite and at left, Billie followed Billy Baldwin's famous dictum: to make a small room look larger, use big furniture, in this case supremely elegant bronze barrel chairs and sofa by Minotti, a surprising departure from the clients' very traditional taste. At near left is Billie's hand-drawn furniture and plantings plan.

ONE WAY OR ANOTHER
KIM HOYT

Kim Hoyt's path to landscape architecture began in the mid-1980s at the Cooper Union School of Architecture in Manhattan. The architecture faculty anchored their teaching in the theory and practice of the Bauhaus. The German architect Walter Gropius, who founded the Bauhaus in Weimar in 1919, wrote *The Bauhaus Manifesto* that same year. Gropius's first sentence is exultant, declaring, "The ultimate aim of all visual arts is the complete building!"

Cooper's School of Architecture, chaired by John Hejduk, included such luminaries as Peter Eisenman, Raimund Abraham, and Rick Scofidio, designer of the High Line. These architects anchored their teaching in Bauhaus modernism. The Weimar Bauhaus (1919–1925) extended the stripped-down forms of industrial buildings into other realms of architecture such as houses, apartment buildings, and business headquarters. Painting played a part, with the radical abstractions of Wassily Kandinsky and Paul Klee, both residents at the school. The Bauhaus did not abandon the crafts but included the weavers Greta Stolz and Anni Albers and silversmith Marianne Brandt.

Instead of teaching students how to draft, Cooper's architecture professors, especially Kim's mentor, Sue Gussow, had students draw from everyday life. Their thinking was that they could learn drafting in an architectural practice, but that connecting eye and hand was an invaluable means for visualizing their earliest conception of a project and of experimenting during its later stages. It was also a powerful way to show colleagues and clients their ideas and thought process.

After graduating from Cooper in 1989, Kim began a master's in landscape architecture at the University of Pennsylvania, oriented toward the earth sciences and ecological design. Kim redirected her design process to the historical and current characteristics of a site: geology, climate, soils, hydrology, and indigenous vegetation, as well as existing structures and surrounding infrastructure.

Kim is hardwired from her lessons at Cooper, beginning each project by drawing a landscape to set her vision in motion. "I design my plants first—where the plants and roots should go—in loose gestures," she says. "Once I've sketched out the scope of the plan, I gradually add details, as in a fine oil painting."

The polarity between the gardens in Boerum Hill and on Fifth Avenue brings to mind *The Raw and the Cooked*, anthropologist Claude Lévi-Strauss's 1964 classic. Kim's Hill's Fifth Avenue penthouse can only be the Cooked, a brick-red New York steak, well done. Boerum Hill is quintessentially Raw, nature seemingly overtaking architecture with unobtrusive organic hardscape.

Photography by Dan Wonderly

Japoniste Garden

Boerum Hill, Brooklyn

On the double lot of a nineteenth-century frame house, Kim installed a new double gate in ipe wood, latticed at the top, which opens onto trellised vistas spilling over with vines.

She divided the two joined slots, each 15 feet wide, into an enfilade of three garden rooms. They progress by function, from social life to complete privacy. Just behind the entrance gates is an area for parking, carpentry, and storing the family's kayaks. There, a "rain chain" suspended from the roof gutter works as both downspout and water feature. Its dangling, small bronze vessels were a decorative and functional element of ancient Japanese temples.

Just beyond is the dining area, sheltered by a 15-by-15-foot trellis dense with wisteria. The trellis is tightly organized in squares suggestive of Japanese screens. A smaller trellis across the space frames a wide garden swing and climbing roses.

At the very back is the family's sanctuary, a natural hermitage fortified by trellises and a canopy of native river birches. The spot's intense sunlight filters through a

A series of garden structures form a gateway between the active workspaces at the front of the garden near the street to the private areas in the rear. The first structure is the garden gate, followed by the cedar shed, split into two halves to create a tightly framed view, drawing you through the sheds to the inviting garden beyond.

screen of ipe beams, configured as open squares rather than more-typical parallel slats. Low walls used as seats were made of brick Kim recycled from the old pavement, replaced with dry-laid, irregular slabs of New York's cleft bluestone. Creeping thyme and ajuga ground covers fill the spaces between them.

The flowers in the family's perennial garden bloom in succession. Kim describes them as a tapestry of native shade-loving plants and more-flamboyant imports also suited to the environment. She mixed camellia and ferns with flowering Solomon's seal and plumes of astilbe and arranged annuals in pots, which bloom for a season and then expire in the cold. After close consultation with the owners and a horticulturalist, Kim added "a rambunctious cottage garden" at the back, swirling with ferns and summer- and fall-flowering anemones, roses, camellia, and wisteria.

To retain some maturity in the garden, Kim preserved and protected an inconvenient ancestor—a giant peach tree with prominent spreading roots. Her client discovered a humbler landmark in the backyard—an outhouse buried beneath at least a century of soil. A team of urban archeologists excavated the site, dredging up layers of artifacts that dated back to the construction of the house, like a timeline in reverse. The spoils included ancient medicine bottles, a hundred years of ornate commercial labels, sleek art deco powder compacts, patterned china, and iron kitchen utensils and garden tools.

Kim keeps the age of her gardens secret; they are beauties who keep admirers guessing. "Ripeness is all," proclaims Edgar in *King Lear*. Kim's passionately realized garden at Boerum Hill answers Shakespeare's plangent call for life to be endured yet enjoyed to the hilt, even as it wanes.

The rear of the garden is the most secluded and intimate area, enclosed by a canopy of native river birches and the two trellises. Low seat walls are constructed of recycled brick (found on-site, formerly used as paving) and dry-laid, natural-cleft bluestone. All of the stone paving is set on a permeable base with ground covers planted between the wide joints. Hydrangea, ferns, summer and fall flowering anemones, roses, camellia, and wisteria all were selected in close consultation with a horticulturist and the client (who is a plant lover and avid gardener). The plantings embed a rambunctious cottage garden within a tranquil, shaded woodland.

Tucked behind the clients' home, a trellis
provides shade and privacy over the dining
area while supporting clamoring vines of
wisteria. A smaller, complementary trellis
sits directly opposite, supporting a garden
swing and climbing roses.

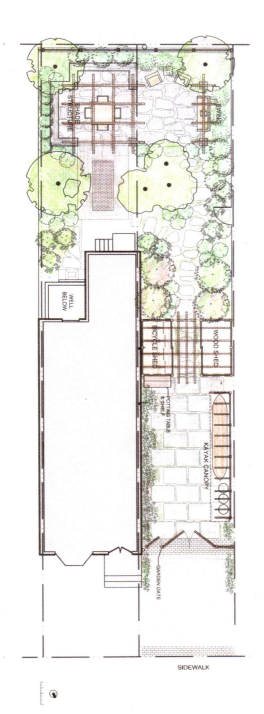

WELL
BELOW

SHADE STRUCTURE

SWING

BICYCLE SHED

WOOD SHED

POTTING TABLE & SHELF

KAYAK CANOPY

GARDEN GATE

SIDEWALK

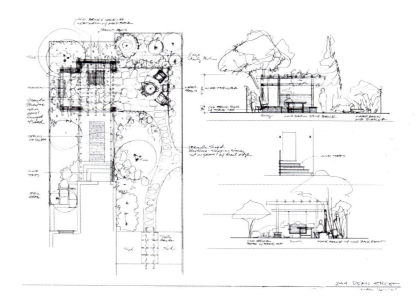

244 DEAN STREET

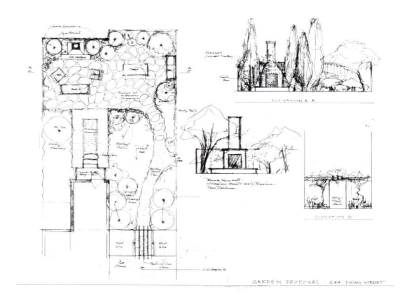

GARDEN PROPOSAL 244 DEAN STREET

Penthouse Garden

Fifth Avenue

In this singular project, Kim did not produce the proverbial marriage of house to garden that landscape architects idealize. Instead, she was go-between for an indissoluble folie à deux. The garden, atop a 1929 building clothed in dark-red brick, runs alongside the clients' eleventh-floor penthouse apartment like a faithful companion.

The south side of the penthouse is a brick structure taller than the rest of the building, too grand to be a garret, too hard edged for an aerie. The same red brick covers the slanting roof, almost a gable, with a tall brick chimney.

The unusual continuity of brickwork resembles the wonderful apartment complexes designed between 1910 and 1930 by the expressionist architects of the Amsterdam school—Hendrik Petrus Berlage, Gerrit Rietveld, J. J. P. Oud, and Theo van Doesburg—who blanketed even their most-eccentric curves in brick. Their buildings, most designed as workers' housing, look remarkably modern today.

Kim's client is a serious collector of Danish modern furniture, that country's answer to the shocking colors and curves of postwar American furniture. America's

Bordering the rooftop edge, *at left*, are five long planters of ipe wood perched on legs, custom-designed by Kim to complement the midcentury Danish wooden furniture her client collects. Kim chose a plant palette of primary red, yellow, and blue—notably poppies, coreopsis, and blue sage—to relate to a painting by Frank Stella in the clients' living room.

seminal designers—Charles and Ray Eames, Florence Knoll, Harry Bertoia, and George Nelson, among others—escaped geometry and gravity by using radically mutable new plastics, cements, fiberglass, and metals. Danish designers, led by Arne Jacobsen and Hans Wegner, continued staunchly to work in wood, especially teak.

Along the perimeter are Sango Kaku Japanese maples in five massive custom wooden planters perched on legs. Kim also sourced twenty "hourglass" planters of all sizes by the Swiss designer Willy Gühl. Commissioned in 1951 by the Swiss firm Eternit, Gühl's chalky-white planters are made of two cones of hollow concrete, one inverted on top of the other. The pointed ends are cinctured together, like the wasp-waisted dresses of that decade. Kim arranged all twenty close together at one end of the terrace, like a jaunty horde of extraterrestrials who landed in Chelsea by chance.

Kim's trees, grasses, and flowers have the last word, silencing even the sirens of midcentury modern design. Of the dialogue between landscape and architecture, she concludes, "Plants, which are the reason for the whole system, are its most ephemeral, perishable element."

Kim works to preserve the fragile, poetic lives of plants, a trust she keeps with equal parts exactitude and ardor.

At left, a café table and chairs are surrounded by Swiss designer Willy Gühl's signature white hourglass-shaped planters, first produced in 1951. *Above*, a long perspective of the planters and brick paving.

Previous spread, ten white Gühl planters of various sizes are lined up against the balcony. *Above*, patio furniture by Russell Woodard, his primary metier in the 1950s. Some of his pieces were of spun fiberglass, or, as in the sofa and chairs here, made of sensuously curved black iron mesh. The oblong coffee table is by Woodard's kindred designer Harry Bertoia, its wooden top replaced with ipe wood for outdoor use. The flared cylindrical white planters in the background are new, by Architectural Pottery.

DIPTYCH
DAVID KELLY
REES ROBERTS + PARTNERS

For a well-worn Manhattan plot awaiting a garden, the arrival of landscape architect David Kelly is like rain after a long design drought.

"You don't just stick a building into an environment," says David. Accordingly, when David first sees a site, he studies it minutely, drawing on his intuition as well as his knowledge of earth sciences and other determinants of a place. What traces remain of its earliest geology and layered centuries of use? How does a plot of earth interlock with the house it adjoins, and with the ephemera and eternities of New York City? To paraphrase the title of Gauguin's famous painting, "Where did it come from; who is it; where is it going?"

Growing up in a rural, ill-fitting sportive town outside Vancouver, David, like so many creatives, had a teacher-mentor in high school, Mrs. Kennedy, who taught drama and art. She recognized in David an uncommon destiny. "You should go to New York," she said. "There you will find your life."

And so he did. For fifteen years David has been a partner and head of the landscape studio at RRP, the landscape and interiors firm founded in 2007 by Lucien Rees-Roberts, then a partner at Steven Harris Architects. The two firms often collaborate. David and Steven work together on projects from start to finish, attuning Steven's re-vision of houses to David's invention of gardens, and vice versa. "An interior and a landscape are not disparate parts," David explains. "They are two halves who talk to each other. What is the couch saying to the garden?"

Photography: Fox-Nahem, except where noted

West 11th Street Townhouse

In collaboration with the interior design firm Fox-Nahem, Steven redesigned the interior of a four-story 1840s Greek Revival townhouse on West 11th Street. The front facade of the house, of red brick with muted blue-gray window boxes and doors, draws a heavy stage curtain of tradition across an ultramodern interior of walls sheathed in expanses of wood paneling, often left to speak for themselves without artwork; furniture arranged in wide open spaces; and, where displayed to best advantage, significant works of contemporary art from the owners' collection.

This interior evinces the influence on Steven and Joe Nahem of Jean-Michel Frank (1895–1941) with hints of Auguste Perret (1874–1954), both of whom redefined modernism by using unusual non-industrial surface materials to severely regal effect. Frank was frugal with furniture and known for his reluctance to throng walls with artworks. But his wall coverings were too wildly original—from humble to precious—to serve as mere backdrops. Frank's wall-covering materials diffused an ambience never quite felt before; they are the *raison-d'être* of his rooms. Fascinated by texture, Frank exalted humble materials—straw marquetry walls, for example—to the pitch of elegance, covered chairs in shagreen and parchment and created novel surfaces from mica, plaster, terracotta, and obsidian." The last touch of elegance is elimination," declared Frank.

The back facade of the house is two centuries ahead of the front, glazed from ground level to roof. Its four levels of floor-to-ceiling windows frame a variety of

Opposite: The back of the house rises as a masterwork of latter-day modernism, a rectilinear tower of four fully glazed levels. The vast windows are framed and supported by tall verticals of blackened steel, including a cage-like structure rising from the second floor to the fourth-floor balcony.

Behind the clients' Greek Revival house, the ground-floor garden unfolds in three assertively modern broad platforms of highly polished pietra del cardosa, a deep-blue-gray metamorphic rock mined near the Leaning Tower of Pisa. Thick white concrete walls enclose the space on three sides, creating a stately court. On the top tier of polished rock presides *Stack* (2015), a 10-foot-high sculpture by Nick van Woert, its boulder-like concrete forms sheathed in glittering copper. The boulders, however, appear precariously balanced rather than securely stacked, with the largest boulder seeming to teeter on top of two smaller ones.

vignettes of the 20 by 30-foot backyard. David described the views as reminiscent of Hitchcock's *Rear Window*, a mysterious scenario one can discern in every single back garden in this book. Jimmy Stewart, laid up in a cast, cannot act; he can only watch. Yet it is this enforced passivity that refines his powers of observation of his neighbors' doings, descending into dark suspicions that set the plot rolling.

The ground-floor garden is audaciously ceremonious, a regal space that transcends domesticity. It is a court, enclosed on three sides by thick white concrete walls and paved in large rectangles of highly polished pietra del cardosa, a deep blue-gray metamorphic rock mined near the Leaning Tower of Pisa. The fulcrum of the square is a 10-foot-high sculpture by Nick van Woert called *Stack* (2015). Its five unwieldy copper-glazed concrete forms resemble boulders balanced precariously one upon the other.

This ground-level garden is minimalism at its most imposing. Against bright white walls, stalks of bamboo rise, towering slender shoots spaced about 8 inches apart instead of in customary clusters. The arrangement is as simple as it is dramatic, suggestive of slender, stately pillars that demarcate the negative space of the walls. The bamboo is rooted in immense steel planters set in a subterranean gym designed by Steven Harris that spans beneath the entire backyard. Along the back wall, the bamboo shoots up through a narrow, trench-like opening that David designed as a light well, suffusing the gym with sunlight. The gap between floor and back wall makes the ground appear to float. Close to the house is a luxuriant Japanese maple whose feathery abundance softens the austere space.

The outdoor steel staircase reconstitutes an early 1950s icon designed by the eccentric modern architect Paul Rudolph (1918–1997). Rudolph had been constrained by the former owners' budget, so he built the stairs in wood rather than metal. When David was commissioned to create a ground-floor garden, the stairs were derelict and unstable. David's work is an homage to Rudolph's singular language of openwork and transparent structures. The widely spaced bamboo rises from subterranean planters.

For David Kelly, the opportunity to landscape a roof garden is "a magical moment." David's rooftop plantings are horticulture at its most painterly. He blanketed the entire rooftop with pink, green, and yellow sedum, a South American succulent ground cover. To achieve this rich composition, David organized the sedum plantings in 2-inch-deep trays, each numbered according to its position.

Viewed from the garden, the house's rear facade is distinguished by a scaffold-like steel structure based on the original by noted architect Paul Randolph (1918–1997) in the late 1940s or early '50s. Rudolph was hired to transform the interior and garden, but the project ended abruptly when his clients divorced. Still, he had managed to raise the living room to double-height and to set a tall, skeletal structure in steel, with the openness of scaffolding; at the outermost left-hand edge of the rear facade. It resembles a transparent elevator with small terraces on each canti-levered level, reached by a cascading external steel staircase that reenacts Rudolph's design. Behind the open steel staircase, ascending Rudolph'd structure is David's long, stately reflecting pool, stretching to the outermost left-hand edge of the house.

Rudolph had built his singular addition in wood to cut costs, and it had all but collapsed when David and Steven took on the project from the new owners. They honored Rudolph by rebuilding his design with details of bronze—the material he loved most. The architect's bones could not quite be interred.

Photo by Scott Francis

For David, a rooftop garden is the promised land of landscapes: "All are a magical moment." On the West 11th Street rooftop, a tiny bulkhead had been turned into an office that constitutes the top height of the house. It is a place for the owners to work and study in private, not to entertain. I am fascinated by the intimate continuity between the office interior, neat as a pin, with its mirror outdoor image where the same orderliness prevails.

From the central glass door of the bulkhead, nine horizontal bluestone stepping stones are flanked by patterned tapestries of sedum, a South American succulent ground cover. The sea of sedum ranges in color from pink to green to yellow, importing the hues of the other America to the East Coast. David organized the plantings in 2-inch-deep trays, all numbered according to their relative positions. An anthropomorphic acrylic birdbath in Thearian green, by sculptor Paula Hayes, epitomizes the sheer exuberance of David's essay in color.

Rooms, indoor and out, are seldom accorded the gravitas of meaning given to architecture. Even the most masterful arrangement of colors, fabrics, paint, furniture; and of vegetation, vessels, and paving, are slighted as surface, seen always as a lesser god than structure. To quote Oscar Wilde, "It is only shallow people who do not judge by appearances. The true mystery of the world is the visible, not the invisible . . . " David Kelly ardently resists this prejudice by bringing to his gardens the subtlest reverberations of every surface, natural or inanimate.

No structure is as enchanted as an aerie—in this case a tiny bulkhead made into an office. From its glass doors the garden unrolls like a long tapestried carpet, bordered on each side by the expanse of a single deep, broad planter patinated in black. Running down the center of this colorful plain is an imposing path of nine horizontally laid bluestone pavers terminating in a paved square for seating. Artist Paula Hayes created the luminous *Acrylic Bird Bath in Thearian Green* (2012).

Photo by Scott Francis

REAR YARD- LANDSCAPE PLAN
3/16"=1'-0"   ①

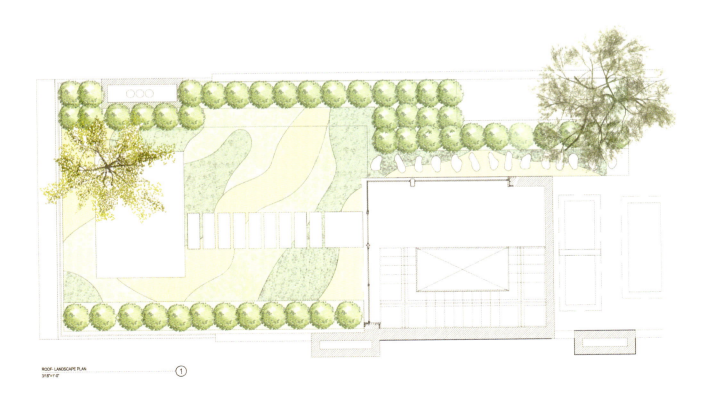

ROOF- LANDSCAPE PLAN
3/16"=1'-0"   ①

LANDED

STEPHEN EICH, HOLLANDER DESIGN LANDSCAPE ARCHITECTS

As director of the Urban Studio at Hollander Design Landscape Architects in Manhattan, landscape architect Stephen Eich lights up the city's dim backyards with shade-loving plants, grasses, and flowers, raising canopies of trees and graceful pergolas to cool scorching terraces and rooftops.

The firm looks to "the three ecologies"—natural, architectural, and human—first enunciated in 1969 by visionary landscape architect Ian McCarg in his classic book *Design with Nature*. His prediction for the future of landscape design has come true with a vengeance: "The most important issue of the 21st century will be the condition of the global environment." *Design with Nature* overpowered the domination of aesthetics in the profession, exhorting designers to look to the natural environment. In the 1960s he led the Department of Landscape Architecture at the University of Pennsylvania, where he exerted a profound influence on his student Edmund Hollander, who graduated in 1983 and cofounded Hollander Design with Maryanne Connelly.

In *The Good Garden: The Landscape Architecture of Edmund Hollander*, which he coauthored with Anne Raver in 2015, Hollander writes, "A powerful landscape unfolds like a story. Your land is your home and within your home is your house." Hollander's declaration is especially suited to his most frequent clients, heirs to immense country estates with grand houses still lived in by as many as five generations of one family.

In contrast to the Hamptons or Litchfield County, New York City's private outdoor land is too rare and too small, no matter how wealthy the buyer. Stephen Eich's clients want gardens that wall out the vectors of nuisance that drive them toward retreat in the first place. But in the city, structures protecting ownership are often more metaphor than masonry. A row of tall trees with wide branches or a running hedge of thick evergreen signals to outsiders "By Invitation Only." They are planted not only as gates closed to strangers, but as camouflage for nearby eyesores that afflict virtually every terrace, rooftop, and backyard in New York City.

Photography: Hollander Design Landscape Architects

City Garden

East 75th Street

Stephen Eich designed this back garden on Manhattan's Upper East Side, much taken by the owners' quiet individualism. The plot, 20 feet wide and 70 feet long, unrolls behind a four-story townhouse, one of four identical linked houses. Built as brownstones in 1881, the original houses were demolished in 1899 and replaced by "automobile stables" completed by architects Hill & Stout in tapestried red brick, now wonderfully mellowed and variegated in tone. The stables later housed a succession of light industrial trades before they were reconverted to single-family homes in 1920. Their distinctive horizontal garage doors and windows, with mullions of blackened iron, are still used as front entrances.

When the firm's clients first stepped into the old red-brick house, they knew at once that their small children would grow up there. They planned to decorate their new home themselves, in thoughtful increments over time.

Tall buildings close in on the backyard on three sides. Stephen camouflaged them by building high walls of treillage painted an intense blue green. A 15-foot dado with a grid of small, square apertures ascends each wall, surmounted by a 3-foot, 6-inch frieze with airier openings. A mirror embedded in the rear wall reflects the garden's expanse all the way to the house's rear facade.

Framing the garden on three sides are continuous low hedges of clipped boxwood interspersed with leafy pachysandra. Raised beds of pink coleus, white-leaf caladium, and New Guinea impatiens border three wide, low steps that lead to a square elevated terrace paved in outsized rectangles of blue-gray stone. It is anchored at each corner by a sweetbay magnolia tree, a species Stephen remembers from his Kentucky childhood. This semi-evergreen keeps its leaves in winter, blooming with fragrant white flowers in spring. Boxy armchairs of natural teak surround a low table incised with concentric grooves.

At left is the richly tapestried brick facade of the clients' house, one in a bank of four houses once used as garages. The bright-pink coleus foreshadows Stephen Eich's vivid plantings in the 70-foot back garden (*above*). This extraordinary view from above reveals the vivacity, complexity, and coloration of Stephen's plantings and structures. His monumental blue-green trellised walls enclose a pleasure ground of intricately layered plants, widely variegated in color and texture. Low hedges of clipped boxwood on three sides are interspersed with leafy pachysandra.

Above: The perspective of the house's back facade at the end reveals the consonance among the original mellow-brick structure, the animated ivy climbing the trellis walls, and the modern yet earthy solid-wood garden furniture subtly incised with rectilinear concentric patterns.

The mother visualized a fairyland within the garden for her daughters, ages four and six. Stephen installed the paved areas with miniature fiber-optic lights that twinkle all day and flicker like fireflies after dark. The trees and hedges are interspersed with ethereal plants appealing to the little girls. Grassy liriope and delicate ostrich fern rustle and sway in front of banks of bright-pink and green coleus. Scattered among them is Stephen's favorite flower, a hellebore with pale citrine petals like pinwheels that reach full bloom in February.

City Garden expresses the refined sensibility the owners are passing on to their children. The family lives there in happiness, knowing it is exactly where they belong.

Rooftop Park

Leonard Street, Tribeca

"This was never meant to be a garden," says Stephen Eich of the field of dreams he made from 5,000 square feet of blank concrete in "TriBeCa."

His design was inspired by Central Park, Frederick Law Oldsted's "four parks laid one on top of another." Completed in 1876, Central Park's areas for distinct pastimes seamlessly cohabit. Multiple paths are dedicated to bikes, vehicles, pedestrians, and horses, while lawns, bridges, and flowering gardens proliferate within the park's 843 acres. "We've taken the lines and gestures of Central Park to create a subtle separation of uses within a single garden," he says.

Stephen's client was an early investor in the luxury conversion of a midcentury parking structure, undertaken by BKSK, resulting in "a vertical oasis" of seven condominiums. At the second floor, a setback terrace for the future "park" was created at the rear of the property, where the new condominium tower rises above the historic structure.

Stephen mapped the "park" into four distinct areas to serve the four uses expressed by the client: a living-room terrace with an outdoor dining area, a small

In the image below, the clients' white duplex condominium is glimpsed at far right; tall city buildings are seen in the distance. The walkway from the living room and outdoor kitchen/dining to the spa is a lawn slightly overgrown with a variety of feathery plants and grasses. Assertively contemporary furniture inside the condominium gives onto the less studied, chronologically ambiguous natural setting.

LANDED Stephen Eich, Hollander Design Landscape Architects

private garden outside the primary bedroom, and a secluded deck with a spa. Stephen chose unique arrays of plants that would thrive in each area's available light.

The dining-and-living-room terrace extends from the apartment's rear glass walls with a view of the entire garden. Paved in white porcelain tiles, the terrace contains a long white dining table with curvilinear chairs. Also on the terrace is a state-of-the-art outdoor kitchen with a stainless-steel professional stove. Kwanzan flowering cherry trees favored by the owner anchor the two corners of the terrace that adjoin the park. Beyond the terrace, the main lawn is bordered by large stands of Russian sage and panicum, a native switchgrass that turns a beautiful bronze red in autumn, bursting with seed heads.

Outside the primary bedroom, Stephen laid out a lawn of tall fescue and blue-grass. Flanking it are river birches that create an overarching allée leading to the elevated spa and pool. The lawn is bordered by low beds of viburnum and shade-loving hydrangeas with lime-colored flowers. In front, a layer of shrubs includes sar-cococca—commonly known as sweet box, a slow-growing ground cover. All are nestled into a field combining Japanese forest grass—a nonnative that thrives with little care—punctuated with tufts of fountain grass.

Opposite: The al fresco dining area borders the raised spa. In the foreground, two large stone half spheres provide a shimmering water feature.

The primary bedroom opens onto a lawn of tall fescue and bluegrass. River birches form an overarching allée leading to the elevated spa and pool. Low beds of viburnum and hydrangeas with lime-colored flowers border the lawn with a layer of sarcococca shrubs, also known as sweet box.

Two views of the spa in daytime, with the professional chef's stove visible at far left. *Above*, the spa by night, lit softly by tall LED candles in lanterns of glass and metal.

From the vista of the allée, one discerns the spa on its platform of ipe, a sustainably harvested tropical hardwood. The shaded island is surrounded by White Prince hellebores against a feathery bed of astilbe interspersed with sprawling Burgundy Glow ajuga, its green-and-white leaves accented in soft pink and burgundy. The delicate array is rooted amid scented fern and Christmas fern. "The backbone of most show gardens is these semi-evergreens, which preserve structure during the winter," says Stephen.

City Garden springs from an early-twentieth-century house and its history, which Stephen sought to preserve as well as reimagine. Leonard Street, in contrast, represents rich groundwork, laid by Stephen, as the basis for the park to acquire a history of its own.

"Creating a garden is like being a surrogate for a child you'll never see again," Stephen says. "You can only hope they are growing up well."

All city buildings obscured, there is a poetic expanse of pure grass, trees, ferns; an exquisitely overgrown space seemingly untouched by city lives.

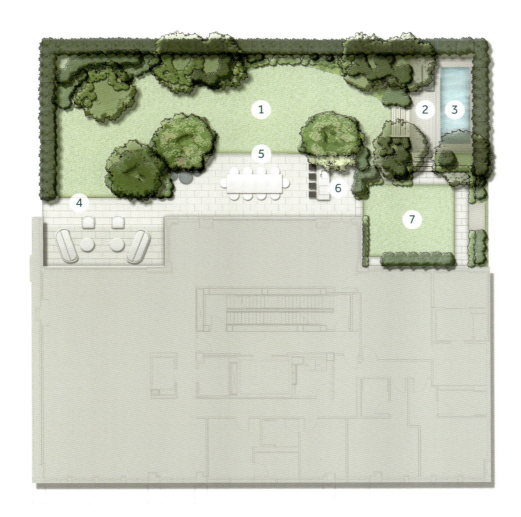

1   Lawn
2   Raised spa deck
3   Spa
4   Living-room terrace
5   Main terrace
6   Outdoor kitchen
7   Primary bedroom terrace

GREEN MANSIONS
MICHAEL TRAPP

Michael Trapp grew up in military towns, where his father would say every year or so, "Don't make friends. We're moving." Michael nonetheless put down roots—in pots. "My childhood was transient, and so my gardens were always temporary. I got my first plant when I was nine, and wherever my family moved, I carried my gardens with me," he says.

Out of habit and passion, Michael wandered the earth, from cosmopolitan European cities to remote parts of Asia. In the early 1980s he studied landscape architecture at Ohio State University but left after two years, part of a gradual exodus of a hundred students from his class. Only eleven would graduate. Michael describes the department's prevailing aesthetic as "the school of broken glass": disquieting, wide-open spaces marred by shapeless totems in concrete.

In April 1990 Michael at last put down roots—"as deep as possible"—in West Cornwall, Connecticut, a gardening nation in its own right. The interiors of his two houses have furniture and objects from all places and times, with gardens of unabashed color and romance. Still traveling the world, Michael searches out esoteric vessels, statuary, and artifacts to incorporate in interior design projects or to sell individually. Many of his clients are figures in New York's art world who live at least part-time in Connecticut or upstate New York, stylish homesteaders, often with pieds à terre and offices in the city.

Photography by Rachel Robishaw

Penthouse Duplex Garden

London Terrace, Chelsea

Michael defines real wealth in Manhattan as "possession of a private outdoor space." His clients at London Terrace therefore qualify as oligarchs!

In 2012 Michael began designing a fanciful garden for a couple's house near him in West Cornwall. The wife, from Brazil, is a fervent admirer of the parks and gardens of the late Brazilian landscape architect Roberto Burle Marx. Michael's country garden for her in Connecticut draws visibly from Burle Marx's wavy outlines of land, and flowing water features.

Years later, the owners called on Michael again to landscape their new penthouse at London Terrace, the Hotel Chelsea's neighbor—more stately and only slightly less famous. The complex, inspired by London's grandest apartments, known as "mansion houses," was constructed in the unlucky year 1929 and opened a year later. It consumes the entire block of West 23rd Street between Ninth and Tenth Avenues.

Above: a rectangular dining area is sequestered by tall hedges; at right by the exterior brick walls and windows of the duplex. The overhead trellis creates an open "ceiling" to the outdoor dining room

Opposite and left: Two views of high-style angular wooden chairs on the wood deck. Michael's overall design for this ultrasophisticated penthouse complex is composed of natural, earthy, even worn materials.

Their 2,000-square-foot duplex—more a house than an apartment—rules the roost of a seventeenth-floor rooftop, one of eight at London Terrace. The second floor of their duplex is wrapped on three sides by a terrace of 1,000 square feet. Michael visualized its long, nearly empty corridors as a nature trail fragrant with horticultural surprises.

On Michael's watch, the empty terrace grew into a hermitage, screened by trees and shrubs in huge steel planters he designed and had patinated with subtle layers of colored enamel. Massed boxwood, juniper, and various kinds of ivy maintain the garden's bones in winter, when the owners reside in Manhattan. The brooding dark evergreens are encircled by the brighter green of delicate Japanese forest grass.

The penthouse windows on all four sides are perfect frames for Michael's horticultural tableaux. "I wanted there to be a view from every window that was

The windowsill is bordered in soft bright-green Japanese forest grass, enlivening a fortress of dark greens: massed boxwood, juniper, and various kinds of ivy.

Opposite: The sheer enchantment of London Terrace, with its red-brick towers and turrets—a rarefied swathe of London's Chelsea transplanted to the epicenter of its New York City namesake.

pleasing to the eye." Intimate garden niches off the main path are furnished in stylish, angular wooden chairs.

As a change from Connecticut's grand historic estates that cover countless acres, Michael loves to visit the small gardens of friends in Manhattan who tend and edit their plants themselves. Soothed by repeated seasons of growth or sleep, these gardeners inhabit a blessed plateau of calm, even during the worst tempests of urban life. "Gardening is the conduit to stability," Michael concludes.

Those words should be cross-stitched on samplers and handed out to every New Yorker, whether their garden is a mock Versailles on Fifth Avenue—or a much-loved plant in a pot.

ABOVE ALL
JULIE FARRIS, XS SPACE

As a child, Brooklyn landscape designer Julie Farris was bewitched by her encounters with the landscapes of modernist homes and open spaces on the East End of Long Island. She cites their simplicity as an influence on the "unfussy" residential gardens she designs today. Into her minimalist landscapes she brings remembered fragrances: the faintest notes of Japanese black pine, rosa rugosa, and dune grasses.

After earning a BA in anthropology from Vassar, Julie studied at Harvard University's Graduate School of Design, focusing on human ecology. Before founding her Brooklyn firm, XS Space, in 2005, she worked with M. Paul Friedberg and Balmori Associates, contributing designs for private gardens and art installations. In 2007 she collaborated with the late Diana Balmori on Urban Meadow, an 8,000-square-foot park, now a permanent park in Red Hook, Brooklyn. Her more recent work has focused on international projects in Rwanda and Nepal as well as residential landscapes on Long Island and townhouse gardens in New York City.

Green Roof

Cobble Hill, Brooklyn

In 2009, Julie and her husband bought half of a gutted 1895 landmarked house facing Clinton Street, in a landmarked enclave in Cobble Hill. In 2012, architects Khanna-Schultz reconfigured the interior. Protected by the New York City Landmarks Commission, the Clinton Street facade was conservatively restored when the front garden was designed.

The only place for a private garden was the 25-by-65-foot roof, 3,000 square feet of concrete. Julie nevertheless wanted a garden as deeply rooted as conditions allowed.

The rooftop is a "beachy meadow in the sky" of abundant perennials, streaked with tall wild grasses. Julie chose vines and other plants attractive to butterflies and nesting birds that bring seeds. "The bees have parties nonstop and invite all the best pollinators—and no mosquitoes!" she says.

Photography by John Porcheddu

This halcyon view of a sublime misty-blue sky meets Julie's complex combinations of grasses and wildflowers in her deep, gigantic "planter," the ingenious facsimile of terra firma she forged on her rooftop. The periwinkle sky illuminates with bursts of sun and cloud the delicate layering of perennials and native grasses below. In the foreground are *Knautia*; at the back are the tall grasses *Nassella* and *Calamagrostis* 'Karl Foerster', mixed with *Molinia* vines, common jasmine, clematis, and Virginia creeper.

Detail of *Agastache* 'Peachy Keen'

Julie wanted the plants on her rooftop "to feel like they are actually emanating from the ground." To this end she created a planter of ipe wood that she installed on the roof, a bottomless box as vast as a playground. Its sides retain the green roof layers, which includes 14 inches of soil. The lightweight soil was placed on the drainage mat at the bottom, formed like an egg crate to retain water and slow runoff. The next layers are fabric, designed to filter the soil fines, and a sheet of fabric stops roots from disturbing the roof membrane. Julie added 2 inches of Styrofoam peanuts for additional drainage.

In the box, Julie planted sun- and heat-loving drifts of agastache mixed with nepeta, gaura, *Geranium maculatum*, *Nassella tenuissima*, *Salvia yangii*, *Verbena bonariensis*, hybrid tea roses, *Calamagrostis* 'Karl Foerster', honeysuckle, and jasmine. "It never ceases to amaze me how happy the plants are, and how tall they can grow in 14 inches of soil!" Julie exclaims.

Julie's autumn palette is cooler, with tall white umbrella blooms of eupatorium mixed with the delicate and taller wild coreopsis, purple and white asters, autumn clematis, Virginia creeper vines, and white muhly grasses. River stones surround a wooden deck and walkway, camouflaging the sides of the "planter." Up on the roof, the landscape feels as anchored in the earth as it would in a backyard, its roots secure beneath Julie's invented terra firma. In the misty distance rises a remote view of Manhattan, its skyscrapers linked in a jagged horizon.

"In Manhattan, most vistas and perspectives are blocked by buildings," says Julie. "But," she exults, "a rooftop garden in Brooklyn connects you to the sky!"

Above: Synthetic lawn with planters filled with *Calamagrostis* 'Karl Foerster', tea roses, and lavender. *Below*, a mix of native grasses and drought-tolerant native perennials.

1 Planters
2 Bulkhead
3 Barbeque
4 Synthetic lawn with ipe wood edging
5 Meadow
6 Skylight
7 Mechanicals
8 Deck

Minimalist Garden
Greenwich Village Townhouse

"The best projects happen when the architect and client know that the landscape designer should be involved right from the start," observes Julie, which was exactly the fortunate context of her garden design for this Manhattan townhouse.

In 2014, the architects Khanna-Schultz began renovating this 1850s Italianate brick townhouse in Greenwich Village. Frequent collaborators with Julie, Khanna-Schultz enthusiastically recommended Julie to their client, knowing that together they would create an exceptional continuity between indoors and beyond.

Julie and the owners talked through three potential designs before settling on a minimalist space "in the spirit of the traditional Japanese garden." The clients wanted a garden room they could live in all year long, sculptural, dramatic, and stylish, yet easy to maintain; an expansion *en plein air* of the spacious sense and sensibility of the house. Julie saw the ground-level folding glass doors and three floors of windows above as transparent portals to a variety of exciting perspectives: from frontal and oblique ground-floor tableaux, to views seen from above that reveal a complex map

Photography by Matthew Williams

Folding glass doors that open from the dining space create a bold frame for the rigorously ordered garden outside. The dining table is surrounded by chairs from the studio of seminal furniture designer and maker George Nakashima; black mesh outdoor chairs are by Harry Bertoia. The small, spherical white stone planters are from Mecox Gardens in Water Mill, New York. Architecture by Khanna-Schulz.

of geometric forms, angles, and intersections, at different levels and heights layered with great nuance.

Julie girded the backyard with sweeping architectural structures that complement those of the house; generous enclosures for "an ecology of natural selection" that requires few resources for maintenance. Julie's layered containers, boundaries, and levels are arenas of change, places where plants evolve naturally, with little intervention through time, weather, and use.

A patio, paved in the same Valders polished limestone as the dining-room floor, extends the interior into the backyard in a sandblasted finish, becoming a low terrace that dissipates into strips embedded in a bed of pea gravel. Its planes of bright white are in high contrast to the dark horizontal ipe fence that encloses the garden on three sides. Dense, disciplined clusters of evergreen boxwood, which remain green all year-round, are corralled in an immense off-center Corten steel planter spanning the middle of the lot to the back of the property. Anchoring the garden at the back left-hand corner is a flowering crape myrtle, its branches dense with leaves spread wide.

Limestone paving from the interior extends beyond the folding doors out into the garden, seamlessly connecting the two spaces. Against a palette of neutrals—a Corten steel planter, ipe wood fence, and natural stone paving—the plants read in high relief. *Nepeta* 'Walkers Low' overflows from the planter at left, and miniature ivy grows from a seam at the base of the fence, trained to climb upward over time.

Into this serene geometry Julie brought an untamed inhabitant—a bold canopy of yellow groove bamboo (*Phyllostachys aureosulcata*)—a plant known for rapacious growth. To contain uncontrolled spreading, this bamboo is contained in a barrier submerged below grade. Above ground, its lush shadowy stalks sways like a curtain across the townhouses looming above the back fence. Around them, the base of the fence is softened by miniature ivy trained to eventually entwine it, and by beds of 'Walker's Low' *Nepeta*—better known as catmint! Small spherical white vessels spill over with mosses.

Julie's abiding inspiration is the Mexican architect Luis Barragán (1902–1988), master of what she calls "the boldness of restraint." Barragán built houses of massive floating walls, illusionistically unattached to ceilings, like walled cities rather than rooms. He painted each wall a different intense color borrowed from the proud flamboyance of flowers. Barragán often called himself a landscape architect, so connected were his houses to the colors and spaces of their natural surroundings.

Like Barragán, Julie Farris builds immaculate structures designed for disruption, by the fervent, unplanned beauty of plants.

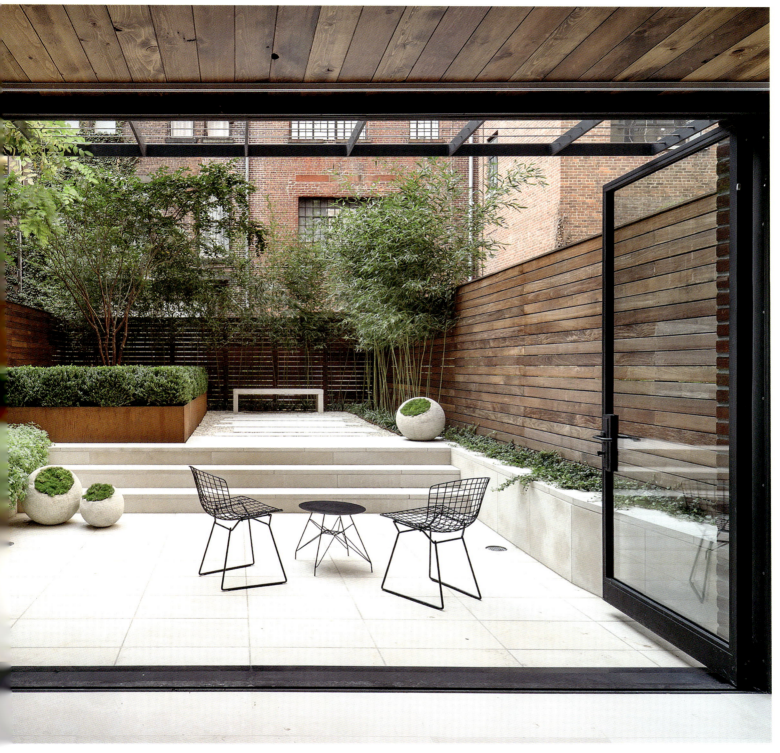

Through a large picture window (*opposite*), Julie's totalized vision is seen in all its nuance, particularly the three steps that rise gently in layers from the kitchen level, drawing the eye up and outward toward the longer view.

Julie's hardscape comprises a vast container of Corten steel planted with a clipped volume of evergreen boxwood. A white travertine slab bench occupies a bed of gravel off-center along the back wall. The incrementally rising steps of sharp, pristine Valders limestone meet the untamed luxuriance of soft, green bamboo (*right*). Anchoring the garden at the back left-hand corner is a flowering crape myrtle 'Natchez', with wide-spreading branches and dense leaves.

Julie's plan (*right*) depicts a series of layered, interlocking volumes and lines. The spacious, deceptively simple layout brings the elegant asymmetry of Japanese gardens to a decidedly modernist design.

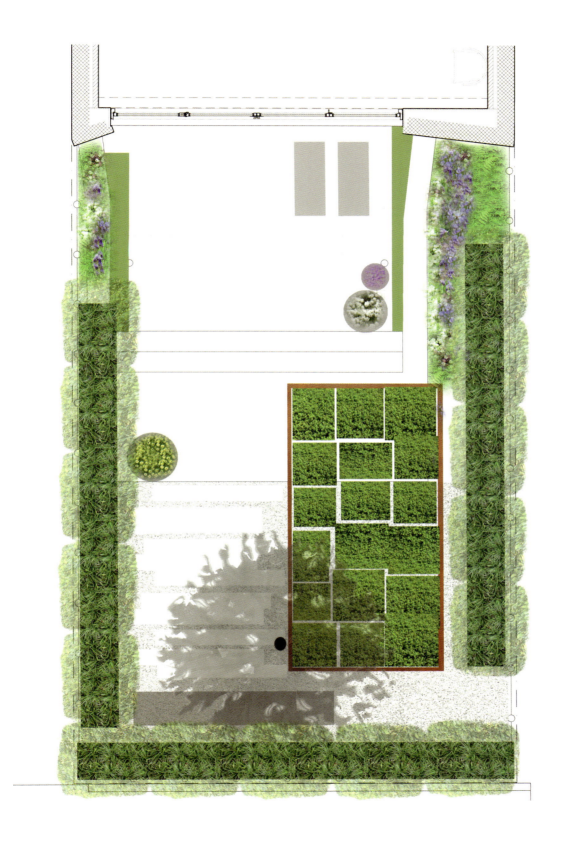

ON THIS ROCK
STEVEN TUPU, TERRAIN-NYC

"When we visit a site together for the first time, there needs to be an imaginary world; a vision that happens viscerally to each designer," says landscape architect Steven Tupu of the process shared by the designers at terrain-nyc, the firm he founded in 2004.

Steven's love of gardens cohabits with his passion for cities. His first was Wellington, New Zealand's small capital city, an intense melting pot. Of Scottish and Samoan descent, Steven grew up with several generations of both sides of his family, all of them mad for gardening. Like that of many landscape architects, Steven's path to its practice was indirect, charmed by detours and avocations that sped him on his way. In New Zealand he had trained as a tailor—"I need to make things with my hands"—an education that still serves him well. In 1991 he was included in a panel discussion in Sydney on the future of its urban areas. The lightbulb of landscape design suddenly lit up in his head. Soon he found himself living in a flat above a shop in the center of Melbourne, a "walking city" of many cultures. Four years later, Steven graduated from Melbourne's landscape school, where he won several traveling scholarships. As if by accident, he became a New Yorker when the second day of a layover en route to Barcelona turned into three, then four days—days that have ticked away to the present.

"There is no reason why low-income housing should not be as beautiful as any other," remarks Steven. Too many older "projects" are streetless compounds of identical yellow-brick towers, cordoned off from the traditional neighborhoods that humanize the hard edges of urban life. The many landscapes Terrain designs for new affordable apartment buildings are now essential to the earliest stage of architectural planning.

Photography: terrain-nyc

St. Augustine Apartments

The Bronx

The site of St. Augustine Apartments is spectacular and utterly unique, built on an ancient, immense rock of Manhattan schist, a cliff on city soil. Steven describes the site as "typical of the Bronx, with the outcroppings, hills, and cliffs so central to the borough." The site has a rich architectural and cultural history; from 1906 until its demolition in 2013, a Catholic church stood on top of the rock.

Steven's ardent desire to preserve the extraordinary setting and architectural traces would become the fulcrum of the entire project. The clients, Catholic Charities, had assumed that the rock would have to be razed to create level ground for building. But Terrain's team saw instantly that the rock must remain as a rare living symbol of the trees, plants, and rock formations that once covered the Bronx.

Catholic Charities was easily persuaded to preserve the rock. Terrain worked in collaboration with Fernando Villa, the principal of MAP Architects, who designed the twelve-story glazed tower with 112 apartments for low-income tenants, some of whom need supportive housing. All is funded in perpetuity by the client, Catholic Charities.

Steven saw in St. Augustine a case study in maintaining a material record of the church, a once-in-a-lifetime opportunity "to peel back and reveal the many histories of the site." A priest from a neighboring church persuaded Fernando and Steven that the new building should preserve traces of the old church, with the new tower a shining "beacon of hope." The original church bell is displayed in the elevator lobby, and garden benches were designed to resemble the old pews.

The entrance to the building faces the rock through a huge window wall with all-glass elevators behind it. Fernando Villa and MAP designed it to be "a place of purposeful common experience, where you are greeted by that view of the rock and its garden elements."

Steven sought to "rebuild" the indigenous plants of the Bronx that had been scraped away since the seventeenth century by successive settlers, but with roots and seeds still there. The rock harbors natural pockets and crevices, perfect for sedge and other grasses. Terrain also planted junipers native to Bar Harbor, Maine—evergreens that thrive in shallow soil, now maturing into cover and shade for the rock.

Woven into the grounds are a series of garden spaces, including one for a community food pantry and a small garden for outdoor Catholic mass. The planted areas are places for residents to socialize, rest stops on the paths to the building and pantry.

On 167th Street far below is a luxuriant border of ferns interlaced with sedge grass. The shade from existing trees works with the new sedge ground cover to produce enough moisture for ferns to flourish. On the long ascent from rock to building, tall native grasses and bright perennials animate the path, thick with *Rhus typhina*, commonly known as sumac—a hardy, shallow-rooting shrub that grows easily around rock.

The St. Augustine Apartments building is literally inseparable from the extreme curiosities of its prehistoric site, an immense rock of mica schist on 167th Street in the Morrisania section of the Bronx. The rock has a mind of its own: heights and depths, plateaus and slopes, excrescences and pits. The entire surface of such features is deeply grooved and furrowed by untold time. Every built element conforms to the oddities of the site, as with this staircase that climbs, curves, and descends according to the steep grade of the rock.

The natural wonders of the rock determined the character of the twelve-story apartment building. Glazed overall, swathes of natural sunlight reach every corner and every resident. The lines, angles, materials, and, of course, the minimalism we associate with modern architecture are implemented here to serve the needs of people, including the need for beauty. At St. Augustine, modernity and humanism meet, in an all-too-rare synthesis unique to terrain-nyc and Fernando Villa, principal of MAP Architects.

"We tried not to be intrusive, and we didn't need to add much," Steven says. Sometimes terrain-nyc's team added soil for more-delicate natives such as *Amelanchier canadensis*, known as serviceberry. Their abundant berries attract birds, along with foraging residents who cook sauces and jelly rich in vitamin C. Nearby, *Myrica pensylvanica*, or northern bayberry, produces inedible berries from its low-spreading, leathery gray foliage. "It's a great plant that does well in bad soil," Steven says.

For the lower terraces, Terrain dramatized the changes of season with the delicate horizontal branches of black tupelo trees, *Nyssa sylvatica*. Pin oaks with short, tough branches are planted near brilliant red maples, along with late-winter-flowering hamamelis, or witch hazel.

St. Augustine's rounded glass corners bring to mind the tall, mannered art deco apartment buildings of the 1930s, when housing and humanity met with sanity and style. St. Augustine evokes the ebullience and prosperity of the Bronx at mid-twentieth century, its plentiful, highly esteemed housing stock serving the means and aspirations of several interlocking social classes.

By night, St. Augustine is exactly the shining beacon of hope asked for by the priest. Soaring and lucent, it is a chrysalis for souls.

A plenitude of terrace gardens appear on the various levels of the rock most suited to harbor social space. They include an outdoor niche for Catholic mass, picnic tables, benches, and a community food pantry. Tall native grasses, vivid perennials, and abundant sumac animate the steep path to the building. Soil was added in various places to cultivate delicate natives such as serviceberry and northern bayberry. The lower terraces are shaded by the horizontal branches of black tupelo trees, along with tougher pin oaks, brilliant red maples, and witch hazel, which flowers in late winter.

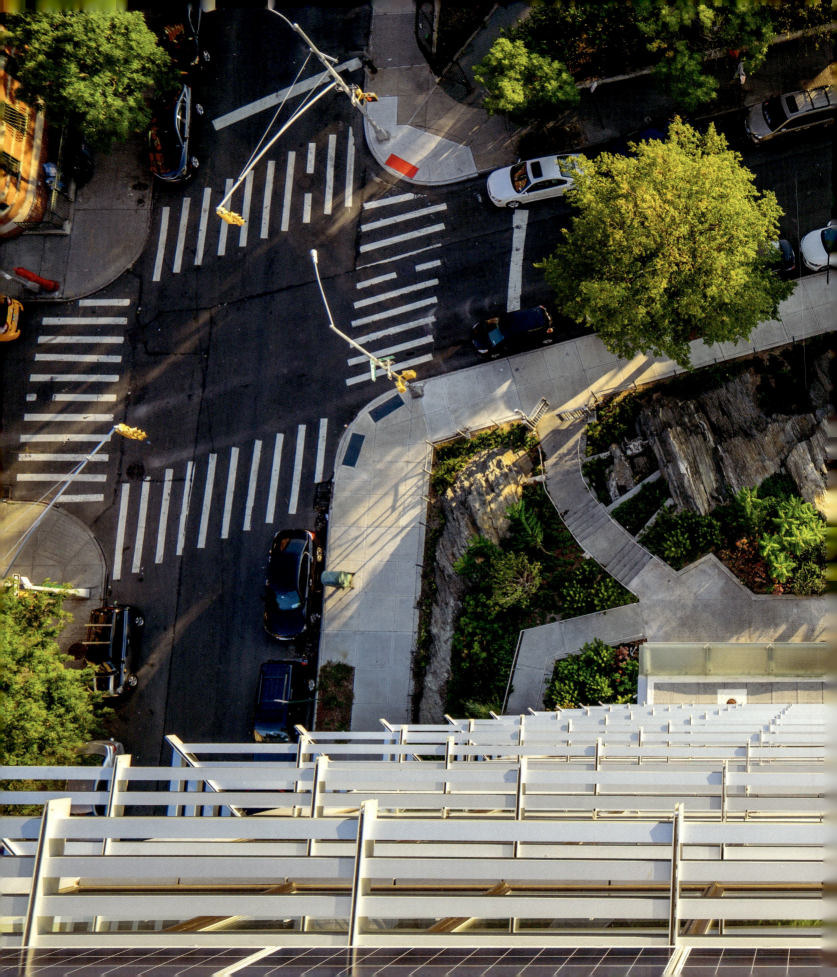

St. Augustine's holistic infrastructure and spiritual presence are perhaps best comprehended from above, as demonstrated by this aerial view that reveals the compound's natural and man-made patterns. The terrace on page 100 contains a precious trace of the former church, a stone relief of the cross enclosed in a four-petal nimbus, elevated on large gray bricks from the church.

THE SEEDS OF STYLE
BROOK KLAUSING

Brooklyn garden designer Brook Klausing grew up in Lexington, Kentucky, where his father, who worked for the city's Department of Parks and Recreation, was referred to as "the tree man." Brook and his brother learned landscape basics from their father very early: how to cut grass, sculpt shrubbery, and plant and prune trees.

Later, Brook became an expert in the masonry, carpentry, steel fabrication, and millwork used to frame a garden, and he still constructs many of the hardscape elements he designs. The slow road of hand building makes Brook's gardens feel grounded. They are places that fuse elegance with easy living. Brook's plans unfold with nonchalance, the ultimate sign of high style.

Photography by Brook Klausing

Rooftop Bohemia
Chelsea

This rooftop in Chelsea is one small star in Brook's constellation of designs, which sparkle throughout Manhattan and Brooklyn. It is a tapestried alley high above the street, colorful in both senses.

Brook designed the garden as an outdoor foil for a charming garret the owners use as a reading room, a tiny annex with a tall, black, cylindrical fire flue and a brick chimney painted pale yellow. The edge of the rooftop faces a massive apartment building across the street, with ranks of windows looking straight into his clients' domain, which is also in plain sight of two townhouse roof gardens on either side.

"We did a lot of work on privacy, but the screening had to look natural," Brook says. "During the hangout season, we like to keep people guessing!"

At either end of the limestone-paved patio loom tall, fixed screens of black-lacquered treillage. Tiny square openings filter sunlight and veil the patio from the unwanted attention of neighbors. Dense, black-green vines of English ivy, a classic evergreen, climb the latticework, delicately interlaced with pale-pink knockout roses. They bring to mind a line from Ezra Pound's poem "In a Station of the Metro": "faces in the crowd: petals on a wet, black bough."

Above the French doors of the reading room, clear cedar beams fan out into an oversized canopy that protects the plants in spring and summer. Directly across from the doors, a row of five hornbeam trees rise from huge angled planters—"troughs" made of gray-brown wooden planks reclaimed from Coney Island's old boardwalk. The trees, in beds of thick sedge, are espaliered against the original iron railing, which runs to the front edge of the roof. A deciduous tree, hornbeams keep their dead leaves in winter, making their wingspan of branches a year-round buffer from street noise and fumes.

Brook liked the "been-there look" of the owners' furniture, which includes a pair of curving black wire chairs, possibly very early designs by Charles Eames, one of them slung with a shaggy chocolate-brown pelt. The yellow leather Butterfly Chair is the familiar classic designed in 1938 by Antonio Bonet and two other architects in Buenos Aires.

The chairs look like they have a past and are about to speak, just like the Beat poets who probably sat in them.

Of this tiny rooftop space, with a small study/aerie at left, Brook Klausing has created an enclave of exceptional charm, characterized by the openness of treillage climbing with pink knockout roses.

The noisy street and buildings below are robustly screened by five tall hornbeam trees, their massive planters made from repurposed wood from Coney Island's original boardwalk. Hornbeam are deciduous trees whose structure and outspread branches endure winter weather.

Garden for a Modern House

When Brook first saw this newly built house in Williamsburg, it hovered over an empty backyard, just waiting to be enriched.

His clients wanted at least one area to be a teaching garden for their children, with hardy, low-maintenance plants easy for them to look after. They also needed a clearly demarcated space for entertaining friends. The garden as a whole was meant to envelop the family in an experience of nature.

Brook divided the backyard into distinct spaces, each with a purpose and perfume of its own. As the garden grew, patterns within patterns emerged. The views from the lower floors became close-ups of subtle gradations of color and texture. High above them is an aerial view of colors contained by outlines as crisp as countries on a map.

Brook believes that a garden must be felt as well as seen. "A vignette is always important, but it shouldn't take precedence over the human experience of a garden," he explains. Into the separate spaces he wove several paths, each one a walkway through changing plants and perspectives.

Near the yard's left-hand wall, a narrow promenade of ipe wood flows toward the back wall. Along its left side runs a low retaining wall, also made of ipe. "A natural cliff," it protects the beds behind it.

Brook clad the upper part of the black-painted stucco walls in horizontal bands of clear cedar. The cedar planks, fastened asymmetrically to the wall, are finished in *shou sugi ban*, a Japanese reburning technique that gives wood a dark, charred surface. On the opposite wall, a wooden bench seems to float, invisibly secured by steel supports behind the wall. The area is paved in cleft bluestone, naturalizing the overall effect.

A second path ascends the grade at the middle of the yard to the back wall. It is built of planks salvaged from the old boardwalk destroyed by Hurricane Sandy at Rockaway Beach. Near the center of the back wall, flat irregular pieces of raw blue slate define a wavy unstructured space with seams of creeping Irish moss between the pavers. At the left side of the back wall stands a small grove of Japanese

For Brook, outdoor furniture is never an afterthought but an integral, mobile element of hardscape and plantings alike. A large rectangular area, paved in big squares of cleft bluestone, has two boxy modernist armchairs reminiscent of Le Corbusier (in fact bought from 1stDibs by the architects and reupholstered). In front of a flanking wall, an expansive wooden bench composed of two oblongs appears to float, invisibly secured by steel supports behind the wall.

pieris and river birch, along with an immense dogwood, an incumbent of the yard. Around the trees are clusters of the sedge grass *Carex pensylvanica*, lavender and gray Russian sage, and a scattering of pale hellebores. In front of a black wall crisscrossed with dark vines of English ivy is a long slab bench, an upended monolith of purest white Delft marble with an interesting pedigree. Salvaged from MoMA's sculpture garden, designed by Philip Johnson in 1953, they were sold off in 2004 to make way for the museum's expansion.

As a designer, Brook has an impeccable eye for architectural materials that are beautiful in themselves. From them he invents hardscaping of startling originality and elegance. He regards these structures, however, as mere plinths for the trees, plants, and flowers that are the substance of his calling.

Gertrude Stein wrote her most famous sentence in 1913: "A rose is a rose is a rose." She and Brook would have understood each other, had they met.

Below, the back wall is a place of sheer romance, brought about by Brook's highly complex plantings: seams of creeping Irish moss around amorphous pieces of bluestone; a small grove of Japanese pieris and river birch to the left, presided over by a huge dogwood original to the yard. The trees are clustered with sedge grass, lavender and gray Russian sage, and pale hellebores. Trained on the black wall are dark vines of English ivy, almost green black.

Below: The yard's black left-hand wall under the glamorous cover of night, with small haloes of lighting. In front is a "natural cliff" of clear cedar planks darkened by a Japanese woodburning technique.

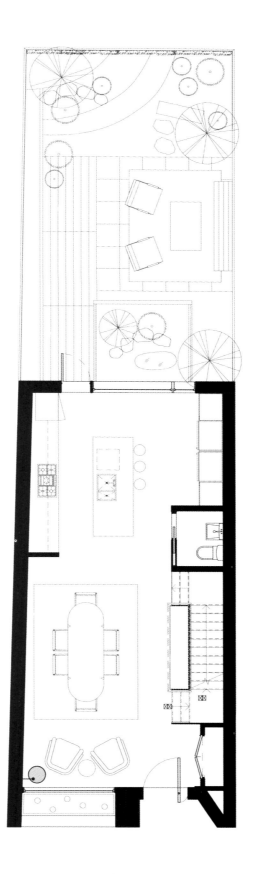

FOR THE BIRDS

THOMAS WOLTZ
NELSON BYRD WOLTZ LANDSCAPE ARCHITECTS

Landscape architect Thomas Woltz is the Alexander von Humboldt (1769–1859) of our time, a naturalist and explorer of every tributary of life on Earth he can navigate—and then some. He commands diverse strata of ecology: agriculture (he grew up on a cattle and crop farm in North Carolina), geology, ornithology, reforestation, water conservation, the preservation of wetlands, and "cultural reclamation." To his direct work with nature, Thomas brings years of scholarship in art and architectural history, and of creating artworks in his studio. Each passion flows into his practice, from immense, very public projects, notably Hudson Yards, to very private ones such as Carnegie Hill House. Since 2013 Thomas has owned and directed Nelson Byrd Woltz in its Manhattan, Charlottesville, and San Francisco offices.

Photography by Eric Piasecki

Carnegie Hill House

Woltz regards Carnegie Hill House as a "vertical oasis." Close to Central Park, the modern townhouse has six stories, with a usable rooftop as the seventh, each garden level dedicated to a particular use. The owners, domestic visionaries, hoped their children would dig in the soil, plant flowers, and learn from the lives of birds and bugs.

Thomas began the project with the unusual step of consulting the head of ornithology at the University of Maryland. He wanted to select plants that attract specific migratory and resident birds, along with insects beneficial to them and to plants. Seed sources and custom nest boxes therefore figured as an important design foundation of the garden. Many songbird species migrate to New York City and sometimes settle, including the house wren, black-capped chickadee, and prothonotary warbler.

Carnegie Hill's stack of small terraces composed natural "nests" to bring together family and birds. Each terrace was to be a fractal of local nature, derived primarily from the ecology of Central Park a few blocks away. He aspired to "expand the domestic realm," connecting indoor and outdoor spaces by equalizing their scale and using similar surface materials in both.

Across the middle of the backyard, Thomas planted a row of 'Princeton Sentry' ginkgo trees, which cut the garden into two horizontally oriented segments. He paved the section closest to the house in large orthogonal bluestone tiles. On the

Below: An overview of the ground-floor garden, garlanded—even swaddled!—profuse clusters and vines in all shades of green. One also sees Thomas Woltz's veritable mosaic "floor" of contrasting woods, and rough or polished stone. *At right*, a closer look, also from above, at the curved "Canasta" sofa from B & B Italia, large enough for a small family. It is cradled by the lacy foliage of 'Princeton Sentry' ginkgo trees planted in a row to bisect the whole garden.

other side of the trees, "woodland greenery" is a mesh of low-growing leucothoe, ostrich ferns, and lady ferns that creep between a pathway's wide black-locust planks. All three of these plant species were found on the site, stored during construction, and replanted in new patterns.

Thomas visualized the entire back wall as an abstract painting brought to life, split vertically down the middle like a Barnett Newman. A green wall occupies the left-hand half, edge to edge with the tall white marble facing on the right. Skeins of dark-green hops cascade down the white marble like Rapunzel letting down her hair into a thicket of ferns. Projecting from the marble near the bottom is a white marble fountain like a long safe deposit box. Michael designed a new minimalist spout—a razor-thin slit that recirculates the water in an inexhaustible flow. Just in front of the wall, a densely planted niche encloses a curving Canasta sofa designed by Patricia Urquiola for B&B Italia.

The small, fourth-floor terrace off the children's room became their teaching garden. Thomas designed a large slate blackboard built into a screen of slats made of teak, ethically harvested and FSC certified. It is one of several rolling screens that interlock, enabling contrasting arrangements of slats. A simple, spirited mix of evergreens and perennials grow in large teak planters that complete the enclosure. The terrace perimeter is secured by an iron guardrail, a safe bird's-eye view of the ground floor

The most startling, imposing element of the ground-floor garden is the towering wall of white marble with a fountain projecting a few feet above a path of irregular stone rectangles seamed with low-growing leucothoe. To the left of the marble wall is Thomas's singular green wall hung with ropes of dark-green hops.

The sixth-floor terrace is a play garden for the children. The sunken sandbox is bolstered at the back by a green wall, a tapestry of ferns, mint, and violet-blue fan flowers. Throughout this "warp" are woven strawberries, basil, rosemary, sage, and thyme, safe edibles easy for the children to reach.

Thomas calls the seventh-story rooftop garden "the sky meadow." Open to the elements, the plantings are domestic echoes of the wild. A row of tall river birches blur the chimneys and water tanks on nearby rooftops. A low seat framed in wood with loose cushions rests against a three-sided enclosure of the same height, an informal boundary between the living area and towering trees, which are underplanted with native grasses and wildflowers.

The poet W. H. Auden once wryly observed, "Thousands have lived without love, not one without water." The white marble fountain supplies water for the birds and a hush of white noise for the other inhabitants. In its steady undertow, every person hears a different song, played without stopping—the soundtrack of a family's works and days.

Below: Thomas's use of variegated forms of joinery, rarefied details that enrich the visual interest of the sixth-floor slatted barrier wall and steps.

Thomas designed an element of particular
charm in the children's fourth-floor teaching
garden: a slate blackboard embedded in the
slatted wooden wall. The chalk drawing is
the oeuvre of the children themselves!

ACKNOWLEDGMENTS

Immense thanks and gratitude, first of all, to Cheryl Weber, my editor at Schiffer. She is the most gracious, percipient guide and companion I could wish for on the long march toward publication. Cheryl saw in my thickets a sure path, with a book waiting at the end, and here we are! Sometimes Providence just sends us a gift. Cheryl's stewardship is mine.

Warmest thanks and kudos to managing editor Jesse Marth. I am so grateful for Jesse's expertise and guidance through the mysteries of production—delivered with a bracing dash of tough love!

"A picture is worth a thousand words," goes the old advertising saw. Designer Molly Shields's layout lilts, flows, and harmonizes the book. Molly made a hundred images sing in unison, all shot by different photographers with contrasting visions. In the end, it is what we see that counts.

Nine lives of gratitude to my closest friends of thirty years and more: Albert Liesegang, John-Paul Phillippe, Andrew Lord, Simon Watney, Stephen Barker, Stephen Bastone, Jerry Rubino, Alan Rosenberg, Fernando Santangelo, Daniel Sachs, Curtis Anderson, Rosemarie Trockel, and Angelique McClennahan. Their voices course through every word I write. I'm still transcribing.

Thank you to newer friends for the long, excitable conversations that so heightened the happiness of writing: Robert Couturier, Wendy Whitelaw, Manny Rojas, Allison Fabrycki, Jerry Znak, Roland Miles, Shirin Neshat, Sylvia Smallwood, Vivian Caputo, Ana Malnar, Simone Perkinson-Harris, Markus Winter, Susan Manno, Alexander Wood, Fatiha, and Farmer Ty.

My appreciation for three exceptional magazine founders and editors: Christopher von Hassett of riotmaterial.com, Sandra Tyler of Woventale Press, and Peter Cusack of the *Cornwall Journal of Contemporary Art*. They are veritable patrons, always open to new subjects and enthusiasms—and to articles long enough for depth.

Special thanks to Tyara Thomas, Shawn Pierre-Louis, Jason Delgado, Alisha Williams, Robin Bryant, Nakima Fuller, Manny Cepeda, Taher Robinson, Lachelle Franklin, and Mike Howard of Weequahic Preservation for their faithful stewardship of Newark's legacy buildings.

All my love to Sparkle Rivera, my beautiful grown-up goddaughter, forever eight years old.

My deepest gratitude and admiration are for Kyle Marshall, who set *Repose* in motion when he so kindly introduced me to Cheryl Weber. Kyle, my much-loved student, teacher, and protector, is that American of honor and action whom one reads about but never meets. I still think he is a thought in the mind of Henry James.

DESIGNERS

Billie Cohen
Billie Cohen, Ltd., Landscape Design Studio
billiecohenltd.com

Stephen Eich
Hollander Design Landscape Architects
hollanderdesign.com

Julie Farris
XS Space
xsspace.com

Kim Hoyt
K Hoyt Architecture/Landscape
khoyt.com

David Kelly
Rees Roberts + Partners
reesroberts.com

Brook Klausing
Brook Landscape
brooklandscape.com

Michael Trapp
Michael Trapp Inc.
www.michaeltrapp.com

Steven Tupu
terrain-nyc
terrain-nyc.net

Michael Van Valkenburgh
Michael Van Valkenburgh Associates
mvvainc.com

Thomas Woltz
Nelson Byrd Woltz Landscape Architects
nbwla.com

ABOUT THE AUTHOR

Lisa Zeiger first saw avant-garde art and early modernist furniture as a high-school student in Los Angeles—not in museums, but in the houses of friends whose parents were serious collectors. At Barnard College, she read and wrote about Dickens, Balzac, Flaubert, Zola, Proust, and James, impassioned by their dense descriptions of houses and rooms. After earning her BA from Barnard in 1980 and JD from Columbia in 1985, Lisa began formal studies in decorative art, first at Sotheby's Education, London, then at University of Glasgow / Christie's. From 1990 onward, she wrote for the *Art Newspaper* and *Apollo*. The decoration of her Glasgow flat became an intense three-year collaboration with American artist John-Paul Philippe, appearing in *The World of Interiors* in 1993. Returning to New York, Lisa became decorative-arts editor of *Nest*, Joseph Holtzman's legendary interiors magazine. Her blog, www.bookandroom.com, is an excavation of every form of visual culture.